For Esme, Clara, Barbara and Sharon

KEEP CALM FOR LADIES

GOOD ADVICE FOR HARD TIMES

EBURY
PRESS

5 7 9 10 8 6

This edition published 2011
First published in 2011 by Ebury Press, an imprint of Ebury Publishing
A Random House Group company

Compilation copyright © Ebury Press 2011

The Random House Group Limited Reg. No. 954009

Addresses for companies within the Random House Group can be found
at www.randomhouse.co.uk

A CIP catalogue record for this book is available from the British Library

The Random House Group Limited supports The Forest Stewardship
Council (FSC), the leading international forest certification organisation.
All our titles that are printed on Greenpeace approved FSC certified
paper carry the FSC logo. Our paper procurement policy can
be found at www.randomhouse.co.uk/environment

Designed and set by seagulls.net

Printed in Germany by GGP Media GmbH, Pössneck

ISBN 9780091943660

To buy books by your favourite authors and register for offers visit
www.randomhouse.co.uk

NOTHING IN LIFE IS TO BE FEARED. IT IS ONLY TO BE UNDERSTOOD.

Marie Curie

CONTENTS

YOUTH

YOUTH TROUBLES OVER ETERNITY, AGE GRASPS AT A DAY AND IS SATISFIED TO HAVE EVEN THE DAY.

Dame Mary Gilmore

YOUTH IS A DISEASE FROM WHICH WE ALL RECOVER.

Dorothy Fulheim

**REMEMBER THAT
AS A TEENAGER YOU
ARE AT THE LAST
STAGE IN YOUR LIFE
WHEN YOU WILL
BE HAPPY TO HEAR
THAT THE PHONE
IS FOR YOU.**

Fran Lebowitz

FRIENDSHIP

IT IS A NATURAL VIRTUE INCIDENT TO OUR SEX TO BE PITIFUL OF THOSE THAT ARE AFFLICTED.

Elizabeth I

**MEN KICK
FRIENDSHIP AROUND
LIKE A FOOTBALL
BUT IT DOESN'T SEEM
TO BREAK. WOMEN
TREAT IT LIKE GLASS
AND IT GOES TO
PIECES.**

Anne Morrow Lindbergh

**FRIENDSHIP IS NOT
POSSIBLE BETWEEN
TWO WOMEN, ONE
OF WHOM IS VERY
WELL DRESSED.**

Laurie Colwin

IF YOU JUDGE PEOPLE, YOU HAVE NO TIME TO LOVE THEM.

Mother Teresa

IT IS THE FRIENDS
YOU CAN CALL UP AT
4 A.M. THAT MATTER.

Marlene Dietrich

WHERE THERE IS GREAT LOVE THERE ARE ALWAYS MIRACLES.

Willa Cather

CONVERSATION

THE OPPOSITE OF TALKING ISN'T LISTENING. THE OPPOSITE OF TALKING IS WAITING.

Fran Lebowitz

A GOSSIP IS SOMEONE WHO TALKS TO YOU ABOUT OTHERS, A BORE IS SOMEONE WHO TALKS TO YOU ABOUT HIMSELF, AND A BRILLIANT CONVERSATIONALIST IS ONE WHO TALKS TO YOU ABOUT YOURSELF.

Lisa Kirk

THE REAL ART OF CONVERSATION IS NOT ONLY TO SAY THE RIGHT THING IN THE RIGHT PLACE BUT TO LEAVE UNSAID THE WRONG THING AT THE TEMPTING MOMENT.

Lady Dorothy Nevill

WORK

I HAVE YET TO HEAR A MAN ASK FOR ADVICE ON HOW TO COMBINE MARRIAGE AND A CAREER.

Gloria Steinem

**NEVER WORK
JUST FOR MONEY OR
FOR POWER. THEY
WON'T SAVE YOUR
SOUL OR HELP YOU
SLEEP AT NIGHT.**

Marian Wright Edelman

LAZINESS MAY APPEAR ATTRACTIVE, BUT WORK GIVES SATISFACTION.

Anne Frank

NOT ONLY IS WOMEN'S WORK NEVER DONE, THE DEFINITION KEEPS CHANGING.

Anon

AS IT TURNS OUT, SOCIAL SCIENTISTS HAVE ESTABLISHED ONLY ONE FACT ABOUT SINGLE WOMEN'S MENTAL HEALTH: EMPLOYMENT IMPROVES IT.

Susan Faludi

IN POLITICS, IF YOU WANT ANYTHING SAID, ASK A MAN – IF YOU WANT ANYTHING DONE, ASK A WOMAN.

Margaret Thatcher

TAKE YOUR WORK SERIOUSLY, BUT NEVER YOURSELF.

Dame Margot Fonteyn

YOU CAN FOOL ALL OF THE PEOPLE SOME OF THE TIME, AND SOME OF THE PEOPLE ALL OF THE TIME. AND THAT'S SUFFICIENT.

Rose King

MONEY

IF YOU WANT TO KNOW WHAT GOD THINKS OF MONEY, JUST LOOK AT THE PEOPLE HE GAVE IT TO.

Dorothy Parker

WHOEVER SAID MONEY CAN'T BUY HAPPINESS DIDN'T KNOW WHERE TO SHOP.

Gertrude Stein

MONEY, IF IT DOES NOT BRING YOU HAPPINESS, WILL AT LEAST HELP YOU BE MISERABLE IN COMFORT.

Helen Gurley Brown

WHERE LARGE SUMS OF MONEY ARE CONCERNED, IT IS ADVISABLE TO TRUST NOBODY.

Agatha Christie

THERE ARE PEOPLE
WHO HAVE MONEY
AND PEOPLE WHO
ARE RICH.

Coco Chanel

WOMEN PREFER MEN WHO HAVE SOMETHING TENDER ABOUT THEM – ESPECIALLY THE LEGAL KIND.

Kay Ingram

MEN

WHEN A MAN GIVES HIS OPINION HE'S A MAN. WHEN A WOMAN GIVES HER OPINION SHE'S A BITCH.

Bette Davis

CAN YOU IMAGINE A WORLD WITHOUT MEN? NO CRIME AND LOTS OF HAPPY FAT WOMEN.

Nicole Hollander

THE ONLY TIME A WOMAN REALLY SUCCEEDS IN CHANGING A MAN IS WHEN HE IS A BABY.

Natalie Wood

NO ONE SHOULD HAVE TO DANCE BACKWARD ALL OF THEIR LIVES.

Jill Ruckelshaus

IN PASSING, ALSO,
I WOULD LIKE TO
SAY THAT THE FIRST
TIME ADAM HAD A
CHANCE, HE LAID
THE BLAME ON
A WOMAN.

Nancy Astor

MARRIAGE

MARRIAGE IS A GREAT INSTITUTION, BUT I'M NOT READY FOR AN INSTITUTION YET.

Mae West

A GOOD HUSBAND
IS HEALTHY AND
ABSENT.

Japanese proverb

I MARRIED BENEATH
ME; ALL WOMEN DO.

Nancy Astor

HAPPINESS IN MARRIAGE IS ENTIRELY A MATTER OF CHANCE.

Jane Austen

A MAN WOULD PREFER TO COME HOME TO AN UNMADE BED AND A HAPPY WOMAN THAN TO A NEATLY MADE BED AND AN ANGRY WOMAN.

Marlene Dietrich

WHATEVER YOU MAY LOOK LIKE, MARRY A MAN YOUR OWN AGE – AS YOUR BEAUTY FADES, SO WILL HIS EYESIGHT.

Phyllis Diller

SEX

SEX APPEAL IS FIFTY PERCENT WHAT YOU'VE GOT AND FIFTY PERCENT WHAT PEOPLE THINK YOU'VE GOT.

Sophia Loren

AN ORGASM A DAY KEEPS THE DOCTOR AWAY.

Mae West

IF YOU USE THE ELECTRIC VIBRATOR NEAR WATER, YOU WILL COME AND GO AT THE SAME TIME.

Louise Sammons

THE DIFFERENCE BETWEEN PORNOGRAPHY AND EROTICA IS LIGHTING.

Gloria Leonard

I HAVEN'T TRUSTED
POLLS SINCE I READ
THAT 62 PERCENT OF
WOMEN HAD AFFAIRS
DURING THEIR LUNCH
HOUR. I'VE NEVER MET
A WOMAN IN MY LIFE
WHO WOULD GIVE UP
LUNCH FOR SEX.

Erma Bombeck

MOTHERHOOD

SOME ARE KISSING MOTHERS AND SOME ARE SCOLDING MOTHERS, BUT IT IS LOVE JUST THE SAME – AND MOST MOTHERS KISS AND SCOLD TOGETHER.

Pearl Buck

DEATH AND TAXES AND CHILDBIRTH! THERE'S NEVER A CONVENIENT TIME FOR ANY OF THEM.

Margaret Mitchell

NO MATTER HOW OLD A MOTHER IS, SHE WATCHES HER MIDDLE-AGED CHILDREN FOR SIGNS OF IMPROVEMENT.

Florida Scott-Maxwell

THE JOYS OF MOTHERHOOD ARE NEVER FULLY EXPERIENCED UNTIL THE CHILDREN ARE IN BED.

Anon

CHILDREN

NEVER LEND YOUR CAR TO ANYONE TO WHOM YOU HAVE GIVEN BIRTH.

Erma Bombeck

THERE IS ONLY ONE PRETTY CHILD IN THE WORLD, AND EVERY MOTHER HAS IT.

Chinese proverb

DO NOT, ON A RAINY
DAY, ASK YOUR CHILD
WHAT HE FEELS LIKE
DOING, BECAUSE I
ASSURE YOU THAT
WHAT HE FEELS LIKE
DOING, YOU WON'T
FEEL LIKE WATCHING.

Fran Lebowitz

LOVING A CHILD DOESN'T MEAN GIVING IN TO ALL HIS WHIMS; TO LOVE HIM IS TO BRING OUT THE BEST IN HIM, TO TEACH HIM TO LOVE WHAT IS DIFFICULT.

Nadia Boulanger

CHILDREN ARE OUR SECOND CHANCE TO HAVE A GREAT PARENT–CHILD RELATIONSHIP.

Laura Schlessinger

THE FINEST INHERITANCE YOU CAN GIVE TO A CHILD IS TO ALLOW IT TO MAKE ITS OWN WAY, COMPLETELY ON ITS OWN FEET.

Isadora Duncan

YOU SEE MUCH MORE OF YOUR CHILDREN ONCE THEY LEAVE HOME.

Lucille Ball

FAMILY

**CALL IT A CLAN,
CALL IT A NETWORK,
CALL IT A TRIBE,
CALL IT A FAMILY.
WHATEVER YOU CALL
IT, WHOEVER YOU
ARE, YOU NEED ONE.**

Jane Howard

**MORE THAN
SANTA CLAUS,
YOUR SISTER KNOWS
WHEN YOU'VE BEEN
BAD AND GOOD.**

Linda Sunshine

LOOK FOR THE GOOD, NOT THE EVIL, IN THE CONDUCT OF MEMBERS OF THE FAMILY.

Proverb

REMEMBER, BLOOD IS NOT ONLY MUCH THICKER THAN WATER, IT'S MUCH MORE DIFFICULT TO GET OUT OF THE CARPET.

Phyllis Diller

HOUSEWORK

I'M NOT GOING TO VACUUM TILL SEARS MAKES ONE YOU CAN RIDE ON.

Roseanne Barr

**DON'T COOK.
DON'T CLEAN. NO
MAN WILL EVER MAKE
LOVE TO A WOMAN
BECAUSE SHE WAXED
THE LINOLEUM – 'MY
GOD, THE FLOOR'S
IMMACULATE. LIE
DOWN, YOU HOT
BITCH.'**

Joan Rivers

MY THEORY ON HOUSEWORK IS, IF THE ITEM DOESN'T MULTIPLY, SMELL, CATCH FIRE, OR BLOCK THE REFRIGERATOR DOOR, LET IT BE. NO ONE ELSE CARES. WHY SHOULD YOU?

Erma Bombeck

THEY'RE SURE HOUSEWORK WON'T KILL YOU, BUT WHY TAKE THE RISK?

Anon

RELAXATION

**GENERALLY
SPEAKING,
EVERYONE IS MORE
INTERESTING DOING
NOTHING THAN
DOING ANYTHING.**

Gertrude Stein

FOR FAST-ACTING RELIEF, TRY SLOWING DOWN.

Lily Tomlin

THERE IS NO PLEASURE IN HAVING NOTHING TO DO; THE FUN IS HAVING LOTS TO DO AND NOT DOING IT.

Mary Wilson Little

HAPPINESS

IT IS NOT EASY TO FIND HAPPINESS IN OURSELVES, AND IT IS NOT POSSIBLE TO FIND IT ELSEWHERE.

Agnes Repplier

TO BE KIND TO ALL, TO LIKE MANY AND LOVE A FEW, TO BE NEEDED AND WANTED BY THOSE WE LOVE, IS CERTAINLY THE NEAREST WE CAN COME TO HAPPINESS.

Mary, Queen of Scots

HAPPINESS IS NOT A GOAL; IT IS A BY-PRODUCT.

Eleanor Roosevelt

**WHY NOT SEIZE
THE PLEASURE AT
ONCE, HOW OFTEN
IS HAPPINESS
DESTROYED BY
PREPARATION,
FOOLISH
PREPARATIONS.**

Jane Austen

IT IS ONLY POSSIBLE TO LIVE HAPPILY EVER AFTER ON A DAY-TO-DAY BASIS.

Margaret Bonnano

HAPPINESS MUST BE CULTIVATED. IT IS LIKE CHARACTER. IT IS NOT A THING TO BE SAFELY LET ALONE FOR A MOMENT, OR IT WILL RUN TO WEEDS.

Elizabeth Stuart Phelps

SELF WORTH

DON'T COMPROMISE
YOURSELF. YOU ARE
ALL YOU'VE GOT.

Janis Joplin

NOBODY CAN MAKE YOU FEEL INFERIOR WITHOUT YOUR PERMISSION.

Eleanor Roosevelt

**LET THE WORLD
KNOW YOU AS YOU
ARE, NOT AS YOU
THINK YOU SHOULD
BE, BECAUSE
SOONER OR LATER,
IF YOU ARE POSING,
YOU WILL FORGET
THE POSE, AND THEN
WHERE ARE YOU?**

Fanny Brice

THE WAY YOU TREAT YOURSELF SETS THE STANDARD FOR OTHERS.

Dr Sonya Friedman

YOU ARE YOUR OWN JUDGE. THE VERDICT IS UP TO YOU.

Astrid Alauda

THE WILLINGNESS TO ACCEPT RESPONSIBILITY FOR ONE'S OWN LIFE IS THE SOURCE FROM WHICH SELF-RESPECT SPRINGS.

Joan Didion

WHEN THERE IS NO ENEMY WITHIN, THE ENEMIES OUTSIDE CANNOT HURT YOU.

African proverb

LOOKS

DRESS IS AT ALL TIMES A FRIVOLOUS DISTINCTION, AND EXCESSIVE SOLICITUDE ABOUT IT OFTEN DESTROYS ITS OWN AIM.

Jane Austen

YOU CAN TAKE NO
CREDIT FOR BEAUTY
AT SIXTEEN. BUT IF
YOU ARE BEAUTIFUL
AT SIXTY, IT WILL
BE YOUR SOUL'S
OWN DOING.

Marie Stopes

PLAINNESS HAS ITS PECULIAR TEMPTATIONS QUITE AS MUCH AS BEAUTY.

George Eliot

BEAUTY IS THE FIRST PRESENT NATURE GIVES TO WOMEN AND THE FIRST IT TAKES AWAY.

Fay Weldon

**A DRESS MAKES NO
SENSE UNLESS IT
INSPIRES MEN TO
WANT TO TAKE IT
OFF YOU.**

Françoise Sagan

FASHION CAN BE BOUGHT. STYLE ONE MUST POSSESS.

Edna Woolman Chase

I'M TIRED OF ALL
THIS NONSENSE
ABOUT BEAUTY
BEING ONLY SKIN-
DEEP. THAT'S DEEP
ENOUGH. WHAT DO
YOU WANT, AN
ADORABLE
PANCREAS?

Jean Kerr

EXERCISE

EXERCISE IS A DIRTY WORD. EVERY TIME I HEAR IT, I WASH MY MOUTH OUT WITH CHOCOLATE.

Anon

IF GOD HAD WANTED US TO BEND OVER, HE WOULD HAVE PUT DIAMONDS ON THE FLOOR.

Joan Rivers

MY IDEA OF EXERCISE IS A GOOD BRISK SIT.

Phyllis Diller

DIET

IF YOU HAVE FORMED
THE HABIT OF CHECKING
ON EVERY NEW DIET
THAT COMES ALONG,
YOU WILL FIND THAT,
MERCIFULLY, THEY ALL
BLUR TOGETHER,
LEAVING YOU WITH
ONLY ONE DEFINITE
PIECE OF INFORMATION:
FRENCH-FRIED
POTATOES ARE OUT.

Jean Kerr

THE CHIEF EXCITEMENT IN A WOMAN'S LIFE IS SPOTTING WOMEN WHO ARE FATTER THAN SHE IS.

Helen Rowland

RICH, FATTY FOODS ARE LIKE DESTINY: THEY TOO, SHAPE OUR ENDS.

Anon

NEVER EAT MORE
THAN YOU CAN LIFT.

Miss Piggy

LIFE IS UNCERTAIN.
EAT DESSERT FIRST.

Ernestine Ulmer

MIDDLE AGE

INSIDE EVERY OLDER PERSON IS A YOUNGER PERSON WONDERING WHAT HAPPENED.

Jennifer Yane

ONE OF THE MANY THINGS NOBODY EVER TELLS YOU ABOUT MIDDLE AGE IS THAT IT'S SUCH A NICE CHANGE FROM BEING YOUNG.

Dorothy Canfield Fisher

MIDDLE AGE IS WHEN A GUY KEEPS TURNING OFF LIGHTS FOR ECONOMICAL RATHER THAN ROMANTIC REASONS.

Lillian Carter

PERHAPS MIDDLE-AGE IS, OR SHOULD BE, A PERIOD OF SHEDDING SHELLS; THE SHELL OF AMBITION, THE SHELL OF MATERIAL ACCUMULATIONS AND POSSESSIONS, THE SHELL OF THE EGO.

Anne Morrow Lindbergh

IT IS UTTERLY
FALSE AND CRUELLY
ARBITRARY TO PUT
ALL THE PLAY AND
LEARNING INTO
CHILDHOOD, ALL
THE WORK INTO
MIDDLE AGE, AND
ALL THE REGRETS
INTO OLD AGE.

Margaret Mead

ANGER

YOU CANNOT
SHAKE HANDS WITH
A CLENCHED FIST.

Indira Gandhi

**ANGER AS SOON
AS FED IS DEAD
'TIS STARVING
MAKES IT FAT.**

Emily Dickenson

ONE OF THE BEST
WAYS OF KEEPING
YOUR TEMPER IN AN
ARGUMENT, AS MOST
OF US KNOW ONLY
TOO WELL, IS NOT TO
LISTEN TO ANYTHING
THE OTHER PERSON
HAS TO SAY.

Alice Miller

WHAT YOU NEED IS SUSTAINED OUTRAGE ... THERE'S FAR TOO MUCH UNTHINKING RESPECT GIVEN TO AUTHORITY.

Molly Ivins

ADVERSITY

BIRDS SING AFTER A STORM; WHY SHOULDN'T PEOPLE FEEL AS FREE TO DELIGHT IN WHATEVER REMAINS TO THEM?

Rose F Kennedy

**IF YOU DON'T
LIKE SOMETHING
CHANGE IT; IF YOU
CAN'T CHANGE IT,
CHANGE THE WAY
YOU THINK ABOUT IT.**

Mary Engelbreit

YOU CAN'T WRING YOUR HANDS AND ROLL UP YOUR SLEEVES AT THE SAME TIME.

Pat Schroeder

IT ONLY *SEEMS* AS IF YOU ARE DOING SOMETHING WHEN YOU'RE WORRYING.

Lucy Maud Montgomery

IF YOU WANT THE RAINBOW, YOU'VE GOT TO PUT UP WITH THE RAIN.

Dolly Parton

COURAGE

IT IS BETTER TO DIE ON YOUR FEET THAN TO LIVE ON YOUR KNEES.

Dolores Ibárruri

**AVOIDING DANGER
IS NO SAFER IN
THE LONG RUN
THAN OUTRIGHT
EXPOSURE. THE
FEARFUL ARE
CAUGHT AS OFTEN
AS THE BOLD.**

Helen Keller

BE BOLD. IF YOU'RE GOING TO MAKE AN ERROR, MAKE A DOOZEY, AND DON'T BE AFRAID TO HIT THE BALL.

Billie Jean King

**EVEN COWARDS CAN
ENDURE HARDSHIP;
ONLY THE BRAVE CAN
ENDURE SUSPENSE.**

Mignon McLaughlin

YOU CAN'T BE BRAVE IF YOU'VE ONLY HAD WONDERFUL THINGS HAPPEN TO YOU.

Mary Tyler Moore

OLD AGE

AN ARCHAEOLOGIST
IS THE BEST
HUSBAND A WOMAN
CAN HAVE: THE
OLDER SHE GETS, THE
MORE INTERESTED
HE IS IN HER.

Agatha Christie

IT'S NEVER TOO LATE
TO BE WHAT YOU
MIGHT HAVE BEEN.

George Eliot

TIME AND TROUBLE WILL TAME AN ADVANCED YOUNG WOMAN, BUT AN ADVANCED OLD WOMAN IS UNCONTROLLABLE BY ANY EARTHLY FORCE.

Dorothy L Sayers

OLD AGE IS NO PLACE FOR SISSIES.

Bette Davis

**WISDOM DOESN'T
AUTOMATICALLY
COME WITH OLD AGE.
NOTHING DOES –
EXCEPT WRINKLES.
IT'S TRUE, SOME WINES
IMPROVE WITH AGE.
BUT ONLY IF THE
GRAPES WERE GOOD
IN THE FIRST PLACE.**

Abigail Van Buren

SURE I'M FOR HELPING THE ELDERLY. I'M GOING TO BE OLD MYSELF SOMEDAY.

Lillian Carter (at age 85)

**OLD AGE IS LIKE
A PLANE FLYING
THROUGH A STORM.
ONCE YOU'RE
ABOARD, THERE'S
NOTHING YOU
CAN DO.**

Golda Meir

LIFE

LOOK TWICE
BEFORE YOU LEAP.

Charlotte Brontë

NOTHING IS SO GOOD AS IT SEEMS BEFOREHAND.

George Eliot

DON'T BE AFRAID
YOUR LIFE WILL END;
BE AFRAID THAT IT
WILL NEVER BEGIN.

Grace Hansen

**DON'T WAIT FOR
YOUR 'SHIP TO COME
IN,' AND FEEL ANGRY
AND CHEATED
WHEN IT DOESN'T.
GET GOING WITH
SOMETHING SMALL.**

Irene Kassorla

DON'T AGONIZE.
ORGANIZE.

Florynce Kennedy

DEATH

MILLIONS LONG FOR IMMORTALITY WHO DON'T KNOW WHAT TO DO WITH THEMSELVES ON A RAINY SUNDAY AFTERNOON.

Susan Ertz

THE BITTEREST TEARS SHED OVER GRAVES ARE FOR WORDS LEFT UNSAID AND DEEDS LEFT UNDONE.

Harriet Beecher Stowe

DEATH IS THE LAST ENEMY: ONCE WE'VE GOT PAST THAT I THINK EVERYTHING WILL BE ALRIGHT.

Alice Thomas Ellis

MORE HELP
IS AT HAND...

KEEP CALM AND CARRY ON

SOD CALM AND GET ANGRY

KEEP CALM FOR CHAPS